50 WAYS TO KEEP YOUR LOVER

Linda Thompson

*Do not get married or be married
without reading this book!*

LONGSTREET PRESS
Atlanta, Georgia

Published by LONGSTREET PRESS, INC.,
a subsidiary of Cox Newspapers,
a subsidiary of Cox Enterprises, Inc.
2140 Newmarket Parkway
Suite 118
Marietta, Georgia 30067

Printed in the United States of America

1st Longstreet printing 1996

Library of Congress Catalog Card Number 95-82243

ISBN: 1-56352-306-X

Cover and book design by Jill Dible

To my hero, my husband Mike,
and to my children, Tiffany and Jace,
and to my stepchildren, Kresta and Micah.

*Don't you kids get married
without reading this, you hear?*

P.S. I Love You!

Preface

Use just one idea from *50 Ways to Keep Your Lover* each week, and you will have the most romantic relationship on the block. This book is written for both men and women. Disregard my choice of pronouns and gender, as the ideas will work equally well for both sexes.

The size of this little book was designed so it could be carried in a briefcase, purse, glove compartment, or pocket. Keep it handy, use it often, and your reward could just overwhelm you.

50 WAYS TO KEEP YOUR LOVER

Small Notes

One morning, several months ago, I awakened at my usual time and stumbled to the kitchen, moaning "CAWWWW FEEEE," which translates, coffee. I reached for the pot, and perched on top was a small scrap of paper. It read, "Good morning to the woman I love." I grinned. Next, I reached into the cabinet for my usual bowl of cereal. On top of the box was another note. It said, "Have a great day, my love!" I giggled. I took my usual shower, dried off, and reached into my underwear drawer. Yep, another note. In large letters, I read, "GOD, YOU'RE SEXY." A sly smile covered my lips, and let me just say, he profited greatly that night for his efforts.

Pamper Her

Pack a small bag and hide it in the trunk of the car. When she gets home from work, tell her you have a surprise, and have her get in the car. Take her to a motel. (It must have HBO and room service. A hot tub would be nice.) We all have a little child in us, and a surprise does not have to be big or expensive. She will appreciate that you thought of her enough to do the planning all by yourself. Plus, getting away from home, even if it is in the same city, means getting away from all those little responsibilities, like the laundry.

Carve Your Initials in a Tree

In April of 1990, we moved into the new house we had just built. The Christmas before, when there was only a slab poured, I went out in 10-degree weather and carved LT LOVES MT in a big oak tree that could be seen from my husband's favorite "spot." Christmas morning, I told him he had a present that wasn't under the tree. After all the traditional presents were opened, I asked him to get in the car to go get his last present. I drove him out to the new house site, where I had wrapped a large piece of wrapping paper around the tree. I got out of the car and dramatically jerked the bow and paper away to expose the initials carved in the tree. HE CRIED. He also said it was the best gift he had ever gotten.

Coupon Book

This idea is a treasure, and it won't cost you a dime. For his birthday, a Christmas stocking stuffer, or just for an "I love you gift," try a coupon book. Using construction paper or anything you already have, make a small book about 2"x 3". Bind it together with staples or a small scrap of ribbon. On each page, write one favor you will grant him. Suggestions include doing little jobs he hates, such as washing his car, taking out the garbage, doing his night of washing the dishes, or mowing the lawn. I strongly advise that at least a couple of the pages have completely SHAMEFUL sexual favors! Use your imagination, girls, and do be BAD. He'll love it!

Bathe Each Other

I didn't say just take a bath together. I said, "bathe each other." Start with a slow, relaxing shampoo, and work your way down. Don't rush! We are all so busy now that we forget to take time to take care of each other. Don't be shy, and most of all, don't miss a spot!

Appreciation

In the preface, I stated that each of these ideas could be used by either gender. This one must be used by both, and never, never, never let a week go by that you don't use this one. Appreciation costs less than any idea in this book, yet you will profit more than with any other investment you can make in your relationship. For this reason, I am suggesting a few of literally millions of phrases you should use daily: THANK YOU. You work so hard at your job. I'm so proud of you. You make me so happy. You make me feel safe and secure. We're a great team and you work hard at it. I appreciate you. You're the best (wife, husband, lover). . . . Talk may be cheap, but enough appreciation will buy you a lifetime of love.

Sending Gifts to the Job

I was a schoolteacher when my husband Mike and I first started dating. About three months into our relationship, we had our first fight. (It's been too many years ago for me even to remember what it was about, but, of course, I was right.) Anyway, the next day after our argument, I was standing in my classroom, trying to teach math to my fourth graders, when my principal knocked at the door. I thought that was unusual because he was accustomed to entering the room unannounced, and he never knocked. I opened the door, and Mr. Cross stood there with a bushel basket of the most beautiful, huge, shiny red Delicious Apples. There was a note on top from Mike. I opened the envelope, and the card read, "If one apple will make a teacher happy, what will a bushel do?" HE WAS FORGIVEN! Send a cute gift to work.

Apologize
Come Back Here — Don't Dare
Skip This One!

No one is perfect. We all make mistakes . . . trite, but true. You WILL "goof up" from time to time in your relationship. There is only one thing to be done. Say you're sorry! "Ain't no way around this one, folks." And then, just as important . . . DON'T do it again!

Concession

This is a close cousin to APOLOGY. For some people, concession is even tougher than apology, but it is just as important. It will sound something like this: "OK, babe, I've thought about it. You were right and I was wrong." OR: "Now that I've had time to think about it, I like your idea better." OR: "You know, I think you're right; that'll work better." This, people, is what compromise is all about. And if you plan to be together 75 years from now, you better do this one weekly.

Eye Contact — X-Rated

THIS ONE'S NAUGHTY! Sexually, the most important part of the body is — Your Eyes! Gentlemen, you can have your woman dying to go to bed with you without ever touching her — in fact, without the first word even being spoken. The art of sexual teasing through eye contact is probably the least used but most important part of foreplay. Ladies, I challenge you. Try standing in a room full of people — a party, a conference, a PTA meeting, whatever. Now, glance around the room until you find your man. STARE at him. Give him that ever-so-slight smile, but never stop looking into his eyes. It's best not to try this until the meeting is just about over, because, HONEY, he's taking you home! Guys, try this one, but be prepared — she could get "out of control." Put on that pair of jeans, slacks, or shorts she likes you best in. Now, put on a button-up shirt (completely unbuttoned, of course). Go to the room in your house where your lady is busy and lean casually in the door frame, thumbs tucked in your belt loops. STARE at her. Look very slowly at every part of her body. Don't hurry. She will probably get flustered and embarrassed, but oh, she will love it! Only a small, mischievous smile on your lips is appropriate, but DON'T look away, and don't say a word. This also should not be done unless you have plenty of time! EVERY WOMAN needs to feel admired. The eyes will do it better than 1,000 words.

Rub Back — Scratch Back

It is so important, as I mentioned earlier, to take care of one another. In our fast-paced society, two people who live together so often become just that . . . two people who simply live together. We need some weekly rituals that reaffirm we are one, we belong together, and we care for each other. One of the easiest ways to accomplish this is to play what my family calls "rub back — scratch back." You take turns rubbing each other's back and head and feet. Nonsexual touching is one of the most important forms of bonding we humans do.

Write a Poem for Your Lover

Oh my gosh, Linda, I can't write poetry!" Of course you can. Even if you have to start the poem out with, "Roses are red, Violets are blue," your lover will LOVE it. Your poem, whether it is very good or very horrible, will say, "I was thinking about you today when we were apart." And I know some of you out there are very talented and should be writing a poem a day. The worst thing that could happen is that she might laugh at your poem. She won't be laughing at you, though; she'll be loving you for being so thoughtful and romantic. Ask her 10 years from now where that poem is, and no matter how bad it was, she'll still have it.

Laugh Together

Speaking of laughter — DO IT! Lighten up. How long has it been since you two laughed together? Science proved long ago that laughter makes you healthier, prolongs life, and besides, it's fun.

Cry Together

I have a friend whose husband was in an automobile accident. It left him paralyzed. My friend says they get through the bad times by crying together. If you are yelling at one another over something traumatic that has happened to you, be it medical problems, bills, children, or whatever, perhaps you need to cry together. And then, hold one another. Make each other feel better!

Take Out an Ad in Your Local Newspaper

For your anniversary, her birthday, or just an "I love you" day, take out an ad: Mike loves Linda. Then, make sure she reads it.

Spontaneous Trips

Don't plan everything. If you are so organized that you just have to plan, at least don't tell him. Jump up one Saturday morning and go to the zoo, or the park, or the show, or the botanical gardens. Take a cane pole and go to the local lake to fish. It doesn't matter what you do or where you go. It is just important to surprise him with an unplanned trip. Don't tell him what you are going to do for him all the time. It's the unexpected little moments in life which we remember forever.

Massage

I've said at least 1,000 times that one day, when I am rich and famous, I am going to have my own personal masseuse. I love to have my back rubbed! Well — Christmas three years ago, my neighbor called and asked me to go to the post office with her to help her pick up her husband's Christmas present, as it was so large she couldn't handle it alone. I ran next door, jumped in her car, and off we went. She drove downtown, but not to the post office. She stopped in front of a luxurious salon in town that was famous for having the best masseuse around. My friend grinned and said, "I lied!" She handed me a card from my husband. It read, "This is just till you get rich and famous. Love Mike, Merry Christmas."

Praise

Oh my goodness! Shower me with it. It doesn't cost you anything, and it makes me feel soooooo goooooooood! I know of a woman who constantly put her husband down. She told him daily how sorry he was at his job. He owned his own business, and from what I could tell, the poor man worked from daylight to dark. Strangely enough, he divorced this woman and remarried. I "hear tell" his new wife praises him from morning till night. She tells him daily how brilliant he is. She thanks him for working so hard. Last week, he bought his new wife a Jaguar XKE, white with gold trim. Praise is cheap?

Gifts for No Reason

When I was about 15, we lived next door to two of the most fun people I've ever known, Lou and LB. They were always doing crazy and funny things for each other. I remember one day LB bought Lou a diver's wet suit. Lou took one look at it and said, "LB, you know I don't swim." His reply was, "Yeah, but it will be so much fun to put it on you." By the way, she learned to swim, and they now live in the Bahamas.

Our family calls the gifts that are bought for no special occasion, "Walkin' down the mall gifts."

Buy presents. Buy her a sexy outfit. Surprise him with a sexy shirt when it's not even his birthday. We get at least a dozen mail order catalogues a month at our house. Why? Because my husband orders something out of them for me on a regular basis. Surprises keep the spice in life. Don't forget them! The other thing buying clothes for your lover will do is keep him interested in keeping up his appearance. For example, I'm over 40, but Mike will buy me a bikini again this year. (I believe he's getting senile.) Excuse me. I have to go work out!

Listen

Your lover needs you to listen. Her day might have been a total disaster, or she could have landed the biggest account of her career. Either way, she needs to know that you will be there, ready to hear and understand the good or the bad. I would like to recommend that you go to your local library or bookstore and check out or buy two or three of the books on the market on the subject of listening. One technique which is often discussed in these books, for example, is the art of paraphrasing: Fred says, "My boss tore me up today." Susan's response might be something like, "Was Bill hard on you today, babe?" Basically, you simply reiterate what he has just said — only in different words. It is a very reassuring feeling to know that your lover understands all you try to convey. I care about you; therefore, I listen.

Baby Talk

Oh how silly." You're right. And DON'T do it
in public. But every couple needs to have its own
language. You also ought to have special names for
each other. This is a form of bonding. It is what
makes you unique from any other couple.

Introduce Your Lover

Introducing your wife is a very important form of respect. Learn how to do it well. Even if you do not know or remember the person's name, you should say, "I apologize. I cannot remember your name, but I would like for you to meet my wife." It is extremely rude and will be very uncomfortable for her if you leave her standing there excluded because you have not made the proper introductions. The most important reason for introducing your lover is because it says to her, "I'm proud of you; let me show you off to my friends."

Call Home

When you are out of town, it is imperative that you call home. Don't make him worry. That ringing phone also says, "She misses me!" If you are in town but will be arriving late, stop for two minutes and call. There is NEVER an acceptable excuse for not calling except in the case of an emergency.

Sexual Innuendo

Constantly work on ways to keep your relationship sexual. "SURE — Linda, we have three kids under the age of five. How sexy can we be?" I've been there. I do understand. It is so difficult to wrestle with your children all day, work outside the home as well, do the house work, and then slip into your low-cut sequined gown at 9 P.M., and romantically whisk your husband out for a night on the town. "RIGHT" — I know it is a challenge, but get a baby-sitter once a month. MEN! Getting a baby-sitter is not a job exclusively saved for women. We will share this little chore with you. Fellahs, one of the very nicest things your wife could hear is: "Dear, I have gotten a baby-sitter; we are going out tonight."

Think of little things to do that let each other know, you're not just my partner, you're my mate. Ladies, you might just brush up against him suggestively while standing in the grocery line. Fellahs, try this: In secret, gently stroke the inside of your lady's thigh, especially while you are seated at a table with a large number of people. A French kiss while you are fixing dinner could make dessert far more interesting.

WORK ON IT!

Brag on Him to His Parents

Oh, girl, this is so important. The most important people in your husband's life, before you came along, were his parents. All they want to hear from you is how wonderful he is, and since a husband and wife should never talk badly about each other to other people anyway, it goes double for the parents. Sometimes the "in-law thing" is difficult at best, but if you begin low-rating their baby, you're cruising for a disaster.

Vacation

Take a break. You need it and deserve it. Surprise her. Save $25 a week and fly to Cozumel, Mexico, the most romantic place on earth. I speak from experience. My husband did just that. Where you go really isn't important, but at least once a year, take a vacation.

Special Dates

BIRTHDAYS AND
ANNIVERSARIES

DO NOT FORGET
THEM!!!

Share Your Problems

One of the truly greatest things about being married or having a lover is that you do not have to go through the "bad stuff" alone. Talk to each other. Share. Work on trouble together. I can honestly say that I have never yet gone to my husband with a problem that he hasn't helped me. And even if your trouble can't be fixed right then, I think you will find your load won't be quite as heavy if you'll let your partner carry part of it. We usually brainstorm ideas together, and one of us often thinks of something the other one didn't, and it always works out.

Don Quixote Syndrome

My very favorite story in literature tells of an old Spanish knight who journeys far from home, seeking dragons to slay. By and by he comes to a tavern. Upon entering, he sees Dalcinea, a barroom whore, dancing on the table. Believing she is a princess, he immediately falls in love with her. The incredible part of the story is that because Don Quixote believed so strongly that Dalcinea was a princess . . . she became one.

That which you expect of those around you is what they will be. Tell him he is the best husband on earth, and he will be. Tell her she is the woman of your dreams and the very best wife you could have, and she will be. Expect the best from each other and that is exactly what you will get.

Encourage Each Other's Success

Never rain on her parade! "I think that's a great idea," is a phrase you should use daily with each other. Don't hesitate to make suggestions, but always encourage each other. He will feel more confident to go to his boss with a new idea if you have boosted his ego at home.

Old-Fashioned Courtesy

Please, thank you, you're welcome, excuse me —
These expressions should not be reserved for the
strangers in your life. Your lover should be the one
person to whom you show the greatest respect.

The Little Things

Sneaking a kiss before work, stroking her hair while you watch TV, carrying in the groceries for her, taking him a glass of cold tea while he mows the lawn, waiting on each other, putting down the lid of the commode so she won't fall in, taping *Star Trek* for him when he's out of town, cleaning off the top of the refrigerator because she can't see up there, folding his socks the way he likes them, etc., etc., etc. If you will work very hard on being thoughtful of all the little needs of your lover, all the big "junk" will fall into place.

A 75/75 Proposition

Two of the wisest people I know are my parents. Something they told me years ago was that a relationship cannot be a 50/50 deal. You'll only meet in the middle. If you each give 100 percent, you'll lose yourselves. Therefore, a good relationship is a 75/75 proposition. Thus, you blend together in compromise, but you also keep that part of you which must remain just for you.

Ladies' Night Out

Although you adore one another and you are best friends, you each need some time out with your own friends. Go out with the girls occasionally. He will also want to have his time with his buddies. A good relationship has no room for jealousy. Always trust one another and never give each other a reason not to trust.

Hold Hands

It's never the wrong place or time to hold hands. I've tried to think of any place or any time that it would be inappropriate to hold hands. I'm sure there must be, but I can't come up with one. Isn't that incredible!

Sitting On Anger

Tell one another immediately when you're upset!
If you keep your anger in and sit and fret and
fume, you'll probably give yourself time to think of
10 more things you're mad about. And when you
finally do explode, it'll be over a ton of "stuff"
instead of solving one problem at a time in a calm,
rational manner.

Candlelight, Bubble Bath, and Champagne

My husband had been extremely involved with one of his projects at work. I was worried about him because he hadn't been his usual "fun" self. One Friday night, after having sent the kids to Grandma's house, I gathered all the candles in the house. (I collect candles, so there were about 30.) I also rounded up my largest box of fragrant bubble bath, two champagne glasses and, of course, the champagne. I went to the bathroom and set out all the candles around the tub and lighted them. I read the instructions on the bubble bath box and found that it called for two to three tablespoons. I poured in the whole box. I filled the tub to brimming, and as I heard him come in the front door, I quickly slipped out of my clothes.

He came through the house yelling my name, and when he peeked through the bathroom door, I greeted him wearing nothing but a smile and two champagne glasses. He then said the most romantic thing I've ever heard. "Damn! I've never seen so many bubbles!" We took a bubble bath together that night, surrounded by all those twinkling candles. It may just have been my imagination, but he didn't seem to think much about work.

Forgiveness

To err is human, to forgive divine." I'm sorry, I
had to use that saying. IT'S . . . SOOOOO . . .
GOOD! He's your "KNIGHT IN SHINING
ARMOR," she's your "PRINCESS ON A
PEDESTAL." Forgive and forgive quickly. Love is
worth a whole shower of forgiveness, while pride is
worth not even a tear drop.

Hold Each Other

A friend of mine came to me to confide the sorrow she felt about her divorce. When I asked if she knew why she divorced him, she dropped her head, tears came to her eyes, and she replied very softly, "He would not hold me." There is nothing one human does for another that is so intimate as a touch. If your couch isn't big enough or comfortable enough for you both to lie together on it . . . burn it! Buy a new one (on credit, if necessary). Hold each other when you aren't even thinking of sex. Hold each other when you are. And — VERY IMPORTANT — always hold each other afterward.

Share Responsibilities

Especially if you both work outside the home, share the housework. One couple that I know uses a job jar. On scraps of paper, they write individual chores that have to be done around the house. They take turns drawing for their responsibilities for that weekend. Of course, my idea is to ditch the job jar, lock all the outside doors, close the blinds, and pretend you're not there if company comes, so they won't see your messy house. Then pile up together on the couch with a bunch of junk food, four or five good videos, and watch TV all weekend. But then I'm a real flake! In an effort to get back to sharing responsibilities, however . . . take turns running to the kitchen for more supplies!

Tradition

Send flowers, candy, cards! Why argue with success? For decades this tradition has worked like a charm to spread love and smiles and giggles and squeals. GO FOR IT!

Love Her Family

It doesn't matter if you don't!!! Do it anyway! In many family units, it is a very difficult transition for a child to move away from home and get married. You can make it easier by working on a good relationship with her family. Please try to remember that these people have probably been living together for 20 or more years, and the fact that you have come on the scene will not mean they will fall off the face of the earth. Although your wife should put you first, her family may be very important to her. Anything that is important to her should be important to you and vice versa. Your understanding will make her adore you.

Making Comparisons

M y mother makes better chicken and dumplings."
"My father can use a skill saw." "My ex-wife made
the flakiest pie crust." "My ex-husband is so smart."
BIG . . . BIG . . . BIG   NO NO!

Make Your Gifts Personal

In the back of our house, we have a small den we call "The Cowboy Room." It has rough cedar walls and a small black wood-burning stove, and Western pictures adorn the walls. My husband loves this room, and I've decorated it this way mainly for him. For his birthday last year, I went to a rod iron shop and had them specially make a Western cattle branding iron with Mike's initials, MDT. He loved it! Personalized gifts often don't cost a lot of money, but they mean so much because you spent a little time and thought to do something just for him.

Think Before You Speak

Very often when I want to talk to my husband about a subject which I know will be somewhat controversial, I'll say, "Mike, don't say anything right now; just think about this." Sometimes he asks me to do the same. When we come back together, an hour or so later, we usually will have pros and cons, and it gives us more latitude in our discussion about the issue.

Children

I haven't said much on this subject because a whole other book could be written on loving relationships and children. However, let me say this: I have two children, whom I absolutely adore, and I have two stepchildren, whom I also absolutely adore . . . even though they call me "Step Monster." With a minimum of one million hours each day which must be devoted to the children in the house, MAKE TIME FOR YOUR LOVER!

As hard as it is for me to face, my children are all going to leave home and make lives of their own. If my husband and I had not stolen the hours needed to keep our love strong and independent, we would be lost when our kids leave. It is also very important for your children to see a strong, loving role model so that they, too, will look for strength in a mate. And, finally, do you want your children to be burdened with feeling sorry for poor mother and daddy, whom they left all alone?

HELL NO! WE'VE GOT MEXICO!

Negativity

If you will look back on all the headings in this book, you will notice I have approached each issue in a positive manner. There is no room for negativity in a good relationship. A very powerful time management speaker that I once listened to said, "For every negative statement you make to one another, it takes 10 positive statements to counteract it." Approach even the bad things in a positive manner. Example: Don't say, "You never tell me you love me." Say instead, "I wish you would tell me you love me more often." Build each other up, compliment each other, praise, encourage, help, applaud, love one another.

From Your Heart

SAY "I LOVE YOU"

AT LEAST ONCE

EVERY DAY!

Love Is Forever?

We hear love is eternal, it is the greatest gift on earth, and it can move mountains. It is indeed all these things. What we don't hear is that love is also very fragile. Never make the mistake of taking love for granted, lest you turn around and it's gone. It is a wise person who nurtures love every day. If you treat love as if you may lose it tomorrow, you will probably keep it forever.

Readers' Ideas

Dear Readers,

You would not have bought this book had you not
been a romantic. If you have ideas to add or little
romantic tips or stories you would like to share, send
them to the address below. We will be selecting some
of these to go in *50 Ways to Keep Your Lover II*. If
you wish to remain anonymous, do not sign your
selections. Let me thank you now for buying this
book and for any ideas you might send.

Sincerely,
Linda Thompson
Rt. 3, Box 293
Huntington, Texas 75949

LINDA THOMPSON *is a native-born Texan. She has been a school teacher, residential building contractor and now an author. Her passion for life stems from her love for her husband and four children. Linda believes "Armed with love and laughter, one can climb any mountain."*